Managing Infrastructure with Puppet

Managing Infrastructure with Puppet

with Puppet

James Loope

Beijing · Cambridge · Farnham · Köln · Sebastopol · Tokyo

Managing Infrastructure with Puppet

by James Loope

Published by O'Reilly Media, Inc., 1005 Gravenstein Highway North, Sebastopol, CA 95472.

O'Reilly books may be purchased for educational, business, or sales promotional use. Online editions are also available for most titles (*http://my.safaribooksonline.com*). For more information, contact our corporate/institutional sales department: (800) 998-9938 or *corporate@oreilly.com*.

Editors: Mike Loukides and Meghan Blanchette	**Cover Designer:** Karen Montgomery
Production Editor: Teresa Elsey	**Interior Designer:** David Futato
Proofreader: Teresa Elsey	**Illustrator:** Robert Romano

June 2011:   First Edition.

Revision History for the First Edition:
    2011-06-08   First release
    2011-11-15   Second release
See *http://oreilly.com/catalog/errata.csp?isbn=9781449307639* for release details.

ISBN: 978-1-449-30763-9

[LSI]

1321376188

Table of Contents

Preface

This book is for anyone using or considering Puppet as a systems automation tool. Readers of this book should be familiar with Linux systems administration and basic Ruby. I'll cover the basics of using Puppet manifests for configuration management and techniques for executing and managing those configurations with MCollective and Facter. I'll often make suggestions that assume you are managing a virtualized infrastructure, but virtualization is not necessary to reap the benefits of this software.

Software

This book is focused on Puppet 2.6.1 with Facter 1.5.6, and the MCollective version used is 1.0.1. Because of the very active development of all of these products, concepts and examples may not apply to earlier versions.

Conventions Used in This Book

The following typographical conventions are used in this book:

Italic
> Indicates new terms, URLs, email addresses, filenames, and file extensions.

`Constant width`
> Used for program listings, as well as within paragraphs to refer to program elements such as variable or function names, databases, data types, environment variables, statements, and keywords.

`Constant width bold`
> Shows commands or other text that should be typed literally by the user.

`Constant width italic`
> Shows text that should be replaced with user-supplied values or by values determined by context.

This icon signifies a tip, suggestion, or general note.

This icon indicates a warning or caution.

Using Code Examples

This book is here to help you get your job done. In general, you may use the code in this book in your programs and documentation. You do not need to contact us for permission unless you're reproducing a significant portion of the code. For example, writing a program that uses several chunks of code from this book does not require permission. Selling or distributing a CD-ROM of examples from O'Reilly books does require permission. Answering a question by citing this book and quoting example code does not require permission. Incorporating a significant amount of example code from this book into your product's documentation does require permission.

We appreciate, but do not require, attribution. An attribution usually includes the title, author, publisher, and ISBN. For example: "*Managing Infrastructure with Puppet* by James Loope (O'Reilly). Copyright 2011 James Loope, 978-1-449-30763-9."

If you feel your use of code examples falls outside fair use or the permission given above, feel free to contact us at *permissions@oreilly.com*.

Safari® Books Online

Safari Safari Books Online is an on-demand digital library that lets you easily search over 7,500 technology and creative reference books and videos to find the answers you need quickly.

With a subscription, you can read any page and watch any video from our library online. Read books on your cell phone and mobile devices. Access new titles before they are available for print, and get exclusive access to manuscripts in development and post feedback for the authors. Copy and paste code samples, organize your favorites, download chapters, bookmark key sections, create notes, print out pages, and benefit from tons of other time-saving features.

O'Reilly Media has uploaded this book to the Safari Books Online service. To have full digital access to this book and others on similar topics from O'Reilly and other publishers, sign up for free at *http://my.safaribooksonline.com*.

How to Contact Us

Please address comments and questions concerning this book to the publisher:

O'Reilly Media, Inc.
1005 Gravenstein Highway North
Sebastopol, CA 95472
800-998-9938 (in the United States or Canada)
707-829-0515 (international or local)
707-829-0104 (fax)

We have a web page for this book, where we list errata, examples, and any additional information. You can access this page at:

http://oreilly.com/catalog/0636920020875/

To comment or ask technical questions about this book, send email to:

bookquestions@oreilly.com

For more information about our books, courses, conferences, and news, see our website at *http://www.oreilly.com*.

Find us on Facebook: *http://facebook.com/oreilly*

Follow us on Twitter: *http://twitter.com/oreillymedia*

Watch us on YouTube: *http://www.youtube.com/oreillymedia*

Content Updates

November 15, 2011

- Added Chapter 5, *Puppetry with Friends*, and Chapter 6, *Extending Puppet*.
- Added a section on Resource Chaining in Chapter 2.
- Minor updates for newer Puppet versions.

## CHAPTER 1

Baby Steps to Automation

Puppet is a configuration management framework with an object-oriented twist. It provides a declarative language syntax and an abstraction layer that allow you to write heavily reusable and understandable configuration definitions. In this chapter, I'll cover the basics of the Puppet programs, the language syntax, and some simple class and resource definitions.

Getting the Software

A Puppet deployment comes with a couple of pieces of software. For the most part, these can be installed from your chosen Linux distribution's package manager. Alternatively, you can use the packages or source provided by Puppet Labs at *http://www .puppetlabs.com/misc/download-options/*. In my examples, I've used Ubuntu Linux 11.04, but the packages are very similar in each distro. There are generally two packages: the Puppet package itself, which comes with Facter, and the Puppet Master server. For the purposes of this chapter, the Puppet and Facter package will suffice. When installed, it will include an init script to start an "agent" daemon at boot, which will look for a Puppet Master. For simplicity's sake, we will test manifests from the command line using the `puppet apply` command to begin:

- Ubuntu: `apt-get install puppet`
- Fedora: `yum install puppet`
- Mac OS X: `port install puppet`

Introducing Puppet

Puppet helps you organize and execute configuration plans on servers. This is enabled through a resource abstraction layer that allows you to address the different configurable components of your system as generic objects. In the Puppet view, a server is a collection of resource objects that have a set of particular attributes that describe how that object looks.

It is your job to build a catalog of resource declarations that will tell Puppet how those resources should look when properly configured. When Puppet implements a catalog, it compares the existing resources on the server to the ones that you have defined in your descriptions. It then decides on a set of changes that need to occur to bring the catalog state into agreement with your descriptions. The execution is *idempotent*, meaning that only the changes needed to bring the state into agreement with the description will be made. The entire catalog can be run over and over again without causing deviation from the described state.

These resource descriptions are made in a Domain Specific Language implemented in Ruby. This means that the syntax is often similar to Ruby, but you cannot simply write Ruby code in a Puppet manifest and have it executed. In fact, the language is declarative, rather than imperative like Ruby. With Puppet, you say how you want things to look, as opposed to describing what should be done to make them look that way. It's Puppet's job to know how to make that description reality.

Putting the Pieces Together

So Puppet lets us describe our server configurations and then goes off and does all of the work for us. But how does that happen? There are a couple different ways that Puppet can manage your systems, depending on your scale and needs.

Puppet

The first piece is the Puppet program itself. It's an executable Ruby program that has the majority of Puppet's functionality rolled up and made accessible via the command line. With the Puppet program, you can syntax check your Puppet code, apply the resources to a machine manually, describe the current state of the world as seen by the abstraction layer, and get some documentation of Puppet's workings.

Puppet Master

When we need to apply our Puppet configurations to a large number of servers, it becomes laborious to log in to each machine, copy our configurations to it, and execute the Puppet command against them. We are better served by keeping all of our configurations in a central location, defining which configurations apply to which servers, and then letting Puppet do the work of pulling the configurations from the repository and applying them. To enable this client-server behavior, Puppet has a network daemon called the Puppet Master.

The Puppet program can be run in a daemonized mode by the server init and is then referred to as a Puppet agent. The agents talk to the Puppet Master over client-certificate authenticated SSL and the master hands out their configuration catalog. In its default configuration, the agents work in a polling mode and check in for catalog updates every 30 minutes. This allows us to store our configurations in a central location without having to worry about keeping all of our systems catalogs in sync through some out-of-band means.

Getting Started

Once Puppet is installed, you will have the **puppet** command at your disposal. The first thing you should do is run **puppet describe --list**. This will provide a list of the available resource "types" you have to work with out of the box:

```
:> puppet describe --list
    These are the types known to puppet:
augeas          - Apply the changes (single or array of changes ...
computer        - Computer object management using DirectorySer ...
cron            - Installs and manages cron jobs
exec            - Executes external commands
file            - Manages local files, including setting owners ...
filebucket      - A repository for backing up files
group           - Manage groups
host            - Installs and manages host entries
k5login         - Manage the `
macauthorization - Manage the Mac OS X authorization database
mailalias       - Creates an email alias in the local alias dat ...
maillist        - Manage email lists
mcx             - MCX object management using DirectoryService  ...
mount           - Manages mounted filesystems, including puttin ...
nagios_command  - The Nagios type command
nagios_contact  - The Nagios type contact
nagios_contactgroup - The Nagios type contactgroup
nagios_host     - The Nagios type host
nagios_hostdependency - The Nagios type hostdependency
nagios_hostescalation - The Nagios type hostescalation
nagios_hostextinfo - The Nagios type hostextinfo
nagios_hostgroup - The Nagios type hostgroup
nagios_service  - The Nagios type service
nagios_servicedependency - The Nagios type servicedependency
nagios_serviceescalation - The Nagios type serviceescalation
nagios_serviceextinfo - The Nagios type serviceextinfo
nagios_servicegroup - The Nagios type servicegroup
nagios_timeperiod - The Nagios type timeperiod
notify          - Sends an arbitrary message to the agent run-t ...
package         - Manage packages
resources       - This is a metatype that can manage other reso ...
schedule        - Defined schedules for Puppet
selboolean      - Manages SELinux booleans on systems with SELi ...
selmodule       - Manages loading and unloading of SELinux poli ...
service         - Manage running services
ssh_authorized_key - Manages SSH authorized keys
sshkey          - Installs and manages ssh host keys
stage           - A resource type for specifying run stages
tidy            - Remove unwanted files based on specific crite ...
user            - Manage users
whit            - The smallest possible resource type, for when ...
yumrepo         - The client-side description of a yum reposito ...
```

```
zfs          - Manage zfs
zone         - Solaris zones
zpool        - Manage zpools
```

We'll primarily be concerned with the file, exec, cron, user, group, and package types. In addition to these built-in types, a large variety of user-contributed modules add functionality for nearly every commonly used configuration scenario. Documentation of the built-in types can be found on the Puppet Labs documentation site at *http://docs .puppetlabs.com/references/2.6.0/type.html*.

To get some detail about each of these resource types, you can use **puppet describe type**. This will output Puppet's documentation on that particular resource type including parameters and often usage examples as well:

```
:> puppet describe host

host
====
Installs and manages host entries.  For most systems, these
entries will just be in `/etc/hosts`, but some systems (notably OS X)
will have different solutions.


Parameters
----------

- **ensure**
    The basic property that the resource should be in.  Valid values are
    `present`, `absent`.

- **host_aliases**
    Any aliases the host might have.  Multiple values must be
    specified as an array.

- **ip**
    The host's IP address, IPv4 or IPv6.

- **name**
    The host name.

- **target**
    The file in which to store service information.  Only used by
    those providers that write to disk.

Providers
---------
parsed
```

 puppet describe type -s will give you a less verbose description. This is useful if you just want to know the correct name of a parameter without having to grep through pages of text.

You can also use Puppet to make queries to the resource abstraction layer and return the current state of things on a system. This makes reproducing a particular configuration on an existing system easy when there is a supported resource type. The command for this is `puppet resource` **type name**. Here is an example query using the host resource:

```
:> puppet resource host

host { 'example.example.com':
    host_aliases => ['example'],
    target => '/etc/hosts',
    ip => '10.0.1.101',
    ensure => 'present'
}
host { 'localhost':
    target => '/etc/hosts',
    ip => '127.0.0.1',
    ensure => 'present'
}

:> puppet resource host example.example.com

host { 'example.example.com':
    host_aliases => ['example'],
    target => '/etc/hosts',
    ip => '10.0.1.101',
    ensure => 'present'
}
```

Resource types are the building blocks of Puppet configurations and most of your time will be spent using them or writing new types to suit your needs. Let's start with a simple declaration of a package resource.

Files and Packages

This first statement declares that the package ntp should be installed and that the file *ntp.conf* should be defined with the given contents and permissions at the path */etc/ntp.conf*, but only after the package ntp is installed. You can go ahead and test this out (on a test system!) by saving the above text to *test.pp* and executing **puppet apply test.pp**. When this manifest is run against a blank system, the agent will check for the existence of an ntp package and install it if necessary. Then the file at */etc/ntp.conf* will be installed if it doesn't exist or overwritten with the content specified if it differs:

```
package { 'ntp': ensure => installed }

file { 'ntp.conf':
    path => '/etc/ntp.conf',
    mode => 640
    content => '
driftfile /var/lib/ntp/ntp.drift
statistics loopstats peerstats clockstats
```

```
        filegen loopstats file loopstats type day enable
        filegen peerstats file peerstats type day enable
        filegen clockstats file clockstats type day enable
        server 0.pool.ntp.org
        server 1.pool.ntp.org
        restrict -4 default kod notrap nomodify nopeer noquery
        restrict -6 default kod notrap nomodify nopeer noquery
        restrict 127.0.0.1
        restrict ::1
        ',
        require => Package[ntp],
}
```

A few notes here about the syntax: The capitalization of type in resources is important. You can see that when the resources file and package are declared, they are not capitalized, but when the file resource references the ntp package, it is capitalized. Always capitalize the first letter in the type when you are referring to a resource that you have declared elsewhere, but do not capitalize the type in the declaration itself. Also notice that the package declaration at the top is a sort of shortened form, leaving out line breaks and the comma at the end of the single parameter. The last comma is optional on a parameter list, but it is generally included in the full form.

The path, mode, and content parameters are fairly mundane, but the require parameter is special magic. The Puppet agent doesn't have any innate sense of order of execution when it is run on a manifest or set of manifests. Things will happen in random sequence unless constrained by some dependencies. require is one of those dependencies. The above statement specifies that the file definition *ntp.conf* requires that the package ntp be installed before it is created. Conversely, we could have specified in the package declaration for ntp that it be run before => File['ntp.conf']. Next, we'll look at a slightly more streamlined implementation:

```
package { 'ntp': ensure => '1:4.2.6.p2+dfsg-1ubuntu5' }

file { '/etc/ntp.conf':
        mode => '640',
        owner => root,
        group => root,
        source => '/mnt/nfs/configs/ntp.conf',
        require => Package[ntp],
}
```

The most obvious change here is that we've moved the file content to an external source. We've told Puppet to go and look in */mnt/nfs/configs* for a file named *ntp.conf* and put it in */etc/ntp.conf*. For the moment, we'll use an NFS mount to distribute our configuration files. In later examples, we can use Puppet's built-in artifice for that purpose. It's good practice to specify both file permissions and ownership in your manifests, as well as package versions. I've replaced the ensure value with an explicit ntp package version. Puppet is intended to be used to make configuration changes as well as to ensure the correctness of configurations. You can think of it both as a deployment script and an auditing tool; by being explicit with your definitions, you can be very confident that your deployment will always work the same way. Finally, I'll note that this file resource lacks an explicit path parameter. This is because, in Puppet, each type has a parameter that defaults to the resource name. This is referred to as the `namevar`, and for the `file` type, it is the `source`.

Services and Subscriptions

Let's add a watchdog to ensure that the `ntp` daemon that we've installed is actually running. This will give us some insurance that the proper services have been started, but by no means should it be considered a replacement for a service manager daemon.

I've added a service definition that **subscribes** to the `ntp` package and its configuration file. On execution, this definition will look in the process table for the pattern "ntpd". If it fails to find a match for the pattern, Puppet will start the `ntp` service to ensure that it is running. It also holds a subscription to the `ntp` package and the file at */etc/ntp.conf*. If we later change the config file or update the package version, Puppet will restart the service automatically:

```
package { 'ntp': ensure => '1:4.2.6.p2+dfsg-1ubuntu5' }

file { '/etc/ntp.conf':
        mode => 640,
        owner => root,
        group => root,
        source => '/mnt/nfs/configs/ntp.conf',
        require => Package[ntp],
        }

service { "ntp":
    ensure => running,
    enable => true,
    pattern => 'ntpd',
    subscribe => [Package["ntp"], File["/etc/ntp.conf"]],
}
```

 Make sure to test the behavior of the service you are managing. It may be innocuous to restart `ntp` when the config changes, but it's an ugly mess when you push a change that, unforeseen, restarts your production database.

2.7 update: In Puppet versions prior to 2.7, the service resource would use a `pattern` parameter to grep the process table for your running service by default. In 2.7, the optional `hasstatus` parameter has been changed to default to true. This means that Puppet will assume that the initialization script that is called for your service has a status function that can be called. If you still need to use the process table lookup functionality, you will need to set **hasstatus => false**.

Exec and Notify

Subscribing a service to a file is very convenient, but what if we need to do something more explicit when a file resource changes? I'll use a postfix transport map as an example. When this file is updated, I want to run postmap to compile the *transport.db* file.

In this example, I've specified an exec resource. This is the "brute force" resource in Puppet. You can use it to execute commands and shell scripts of your choosing, but there is an important caveat. The command must be idempotent. This means that your system configuration must be able to cope with having the command run over and over again. An exec type resource will generally be run on every Puppet run. The following example specifies that the command should not run unless the subscription to the */etc/ postfix/transport* file is changed and a *refresh* is triggered. This is accomplished with the refreshonly parameter. Any exec can be refreshed either by a subscription or a notification. Notification works in the reverse of a subscription:

```
file { "/etc/postfix/transport":
        mode => 640
        owner => root,
        group => postfix,
        source => '/mnt/postfix/configs/transport',
        }
exec { "postmap /etc/postfix/transport":
        subscribe => File["/etc/postfix/transport"],
        refreshonly => true,
        }
```

Here we have the file resource notifying the exec of a change. Note that *notify* implies the behavior that would be seen with a before parameter and *subscribe* implies the ordering of a require parameter. In this example, the file will be created before the exec is run, and in the former example, the exec requires that the file be run first:

```
file { "/etc/postfix/transport":
        mode => 640
        owner => root,
        group => postfix,
        source => '/mnt/postfix/configs/transport',
        notify => Exec["postmap /etc/postfix/transport"],
        }
exec { "postmap /etc/postfix/transport":
        refreshonly => true,
        }
```

There are a couple of scenarios where you might want to use an exec, but only when some other condition requires it. Exec can be used to generate a file; for example, if I wish to fetch a configuration file that I've published on a web server.

In the first example, Puppet understands that the result of the exec is to create the file listed in the creates parameter. This exec will only be run if that file doesn't exist. The second example has the same effect, but it does so using a more customizable condition.

The command will only be run if the exit status of the command in the `onlyif` parameter is zero. Nonzero status will cause the exec to be skipped:

```
exec { 'curl http://example.com/config/my.conf -o "/etc/myapp/my.conf"':
    creates => "/etc/myapp/my.conf",
    }

exec { 'curl http://example.com/config/my.conf -o "/etc/myapp/my.conf"':
    onlyif => "test ! -e /etc/myapp/my.conf",
    }
```

Exec is very powerful and it has plenty of appropriate uses. It is not advisable, however, to treat every problem as a potential nail for this particular hammer. An exec is difficult to make platform-agnostic, and it generally solves only one particular problem. In a case where no existing Puppet abstraction does what you need, it might be more useful to dig around in the community modules for an adaptable function. You could even write your own.

Facts, Conditional Statements, and Logging

It's time to begin talking about what Puppet is doing when it executes these definitions. Each type has a set of "provider" backends that specify what to do with all of the parameters we've given it. Each type also has a specified default provider, depending on the nature of the machine you are executing on. In the package definition for `ntp` we have not told Puppet how to install the package or what commands to use. Instead it knows that we are on an Ubuntu system and has a specified default provider of "apt". The providers can be explicitly passed in a parameter such as `provider => apt,`, but this is generally unnecessary and even undesirable. If you were writing Puppet automation for a heterogeneous environment with both CentOS and Ubuntu hosts, it would benefit you to allow Puppet to make the choice.

It's a great habit to write your manifests to be as operating system independent as you can manage. Not only will it help make your system more versatile, but it will make it convenient for others in the community to reuse when you graciously contribute it back!

This begs the question: *How does Puppet know what OS it's running on?* The answer lies with the `facter` command. Go ahead and execute **facter --puppet** and inspect the results. You'll see that Facter knows a lot about your system configuration. Facter comes with a wide range of "facts" defined that describe all different parts of your system. To ascertain what OS it's running on, Puppet uses the Facter library and looks up the `$operatingsystem` fact. These facts are also available to us in the manifests themselves. If we would rather make explicit decisions about what to do in different situations (like on different operating systems), we can do that with facts.

In this example, I've added a selector operation into the source parameter. This specifies that if the $operatingsystem fact is Ubuntu, we should use the source file at */mnt/nfs/ configs/ubuntu-ntp.conf*; else we should use the default source file. Classic if-else and case statements are also allowed:

```
package { 'ntp': ensure => '1:4.2.6.p2+dfsg-1ubuntu5' }

file { '/etc/ntp.conf':
                mode => '640',
                owner => root,
                group => root,
                source => $operatingsystem ? {
                    'Ubuntu' => '/mnt/nfs/configs/ubuntu-ntp.conf',
                    default => '/mnt/nfs/configs/default-ntp.conf',
                            },
                require => Package[ntp],
                        }

service { "ntp":
        ensure => running,
        enable => true,
        pattern => 'ntpd',
subscribe => [Package["ntp"], File["/etc/ntp.conf"]],
    }
```

Here we've made a simple decision tree that prints out a notice depending on the OS type and version reported by Facter. Notices can be useful for logging of Puppet runs and reporting on exceptional conditions. Puppet can be very verbose about what changes it's made, but custom logging is convenient:

```
if $operatingsystem == 'Ubuntu' {
    case $operatingsystemrelease {
        '11.04':   { notice("Natty Narwahl") }
        '10.10':   { notice("Maverick Meerkat") }
        '10.04':   { notice("Lucid Lynx") }
        }
} else {
    notice("We're not on Ubuntu!")
}
```

With these basic tools alone, we have enough to begin writing some convenient system installation scripts. That would let us build up a big manifest full of resource declarations and decision structures and then apply them to a system with Puppet. This manual execution is useful for writing and testing Puppet manifests, but as we'll see in the next chapter, we can let the servers configure themselves instead.

The Puppet Master

Running a central Puppet Master server will allow us to build configurations that are specific to a particular system and then hand them out to be executed on demand. It can be a central repository for the configuration of all servers in your data center, allowing for the centralized deployment of updates and applications.

Once the Puppet Master is installed, you'll have an empty Puppet repository in */etc/puppet*. When the Puppet Master starts up, the first file it loads is */etc/puppet/manifests/site.pp*. Generally this file will include a *nodes.pp* file as well as set some default parameters. *nodes.pp* will tell the Puppet Master how to decide what *classes* it should apply to a system, called a node, when it checks in.

 The Puppet Master and agent communicate over tcp port 8140. Make sure that any applicable firewall settings allow communication on that port between the two.

Let's step through how to set up a node definition and apply a class to it with a central Puppet Master rather than by manually applying the manifest.

First, you'll need to have both agent and master installed. For simplicity's sake, these can be on the same system. Then set up a simple */etc/puppet/manifests/site.pp* and *nodes.pp*.

This *site.pp* includes our *nodes.pp* and sets up a couple of defaults. The first of these is the filebucket. When Puppet makes some change to the filesystem, such as overwriting a config file with an update, it will make a backup of the original. When we define a filebucket on our Puppet Master server (which we assume to have the hostname *puppet.example.com*), we can then tell all the file type resource declarations to default their backup to that bucket. The way that I've set up that default here is called a *metaparameter*. When I declare a capitalized file resource with no title, the parameters I specify for it will become the default for that resource type. I've also specified a metaparameter default for the path of the exec resource type. Exec is used to execute arbitrary commands from the agent and it is convenient to have a standard default path set to look for executables:

```
# site.pp
import "nodes"

filebucket { main: server => "puppet.example.com" }

# defaults
File { backup => main }
Exec { path => "/usr/bin:/usr/sbin/:/bin:/sbin" }
```

In this example, I've defined a node explicitly as *puppet.example.com* and also as a default. The Puppet Master matches nodes based upon their hostnames and will fall back to a default node declaration if a matching node is not found. In this case, either way, the `apps::ntp` class will be applied to the node:

```
# nodes.pp

node default {
    include apps::ntp
    }

node "puppet.example.com" {
    include apps::ntp
    }
```

Modules for Organization

The Puppet structure that stores sets of related classes is called a module. The Puppet Master has an autoloader that expects your classes to be in certain subdirectory structures of the */etc/puppet/modules* directory. */etc/puppet/modules/mymodule/manifests* should contain the *init.pp* file for your mymodule class and any imports it may have. Files that the class will distribute should live in */etc/puppet/modules/mymodule/files*, and ERB templates in */etc/puppet/modules/mymodule/templates*.

Newer versions of Puppet (2.6+) no longer require that each module have an *init.pp* file. The newer method will load classes from any *.pp* file in your module manifests directory and its subdirectories. It is now convention to place each class in its own file of matching name and to avoid the use of imports altogether.

Now that we've told our Puppet Master how to identify our agent and what to do with it, we need to put the `ntp` manifest that we created earlier into the `apps::ntp` class. This way, when the agent runs it will execute our `ntp` installation just as it did when it was applied with the `puppet apply` command. We'll put the class in */etc/puppet/modules/apps/init.pp*.

You'll notice that the source parameter has changed for our *ntp.conf* file. I've defined a string here that points to a place where our Puppet server expects module files to be kept. This `puppet:///modules/apps/ntp/ntp.conf` location maps to the */etc/puppet/modules/apps/files/ntp/ntp.conf* location on our Puppet Master. This allows us to distribute files from the master to the clients without having to jump through any extra hoops, such as setting up `nfs`. Make sure to copy the *ntp.conf* file to the proper place on the master before continuing:

```
# apps/init.pp
class apps::ntp {
    package { 'ntp': ensure => '1:4.2.6.p2+dfsg-1ubuntu5' }

    file { '/etc/ntp.conf':
                    mode => '640',
                    owner => root,
                    group => root,
                    source => "puppet:///modules/apps/ntp/ntp.conf",
```

```
                    require => Package[ntp],
                            }

            service { "ntp":
                    ensure => running,
                    enable => true,
                    pattern => 'ntpd',
            subscribe => [Package["ntp"], File["/etc/ntp.conf"]],
    }
}
```

With our node defined and importing the ntp class that we've written, we can now test out the agent. On the Puppet agent node, run **sudo puppetd --test --noop --server** *puppet.example.com*. This will tell the agent to run without daemonizing into the background (--test) and without actually modifying anything (--noop). The first run will not obtain a configuration from the Puppet Master because the agent has not yet been authenticated. It did, however, leave its certificate on the master for inspection. The next step in getting our agent and master talking is to have the Puppet Master sign our agent's SSL certificate. This initial authentication step is done with the puppetca command. On the Puppet Master, run **sudo puppetca -la**. This will list all of the certificates in our Puppet Master's certificate store. Certificates that are signed will have a + in front of them, and unsigned certificates will not. You should see a certificate for your agent that is not yet signed. To sign it, simply run **sudo puppetca -sa**. This will sign all the outstanding requests and allow those agents to talk to the master.

You can define client node names in the */etc/puppet/autosign.conf* file in the format *agenthost.example.com* or even **.example.com*. Names matching these patterns will be signed automatically by the master.

At this point, we should have a fully functional master and agent pair. The client certificate is signed, the node has a definition, and there is a class for the ntp installation assigned to it. Let's prove that it works by running **sudo puppetd --test --server** *puppet.example.com* on our client. You should see the agent run through our manifest and install ntp.

Congratulations, you've taken a big step toward implementing a scalable configuration management architecture. Some deployments will need more complicated logic than packages and configuration files, but there are plenty of resource types, plug-ins, and examples to help you out. In the next chapter, we'll look at the more advanced features of Puppet that will let you take these simple configuration definitions and apply them in a larger-scale fashion.

Puppet in the Ubuntu Cloud

If you're using Ubuntu virtual images (on Amazon AWS or Ubuntu Enterprise Cloud), you will have a neat feature called cloud-init. Cloud-init provides a boot hook that can consume data from an input on instance launch and do things like install packages or execute scripts. On your instance there will be an example at *usr/share/doc/cloud-init/ examples/cloud-config-puppet.txt* that describes how to install Puppet at boot and contact a Puppet Master:

```
puppet:
    conf:
        agent:
            server: "puppetmaster.example.com"
            certname: "myinstance.example.com"
```

At the simplest, all that needs to be specified in this file is your Puppet server and the node name to identify the new instance (cert name).

## CHAPTER 2

Puppeteering

Before we can get into a full-scale example, we need to add more tools to our Puppet workbench. Puppet provides several layers of abstraction to give you a variety of options for structuring configurations.

Defines

In this example, I've defined a type called `yellifmissing`, which takes a parameter `$path`. Then I can instantiate an instance of `yellifmissing` called `pathnumber1` and pass the path parameter */tmp/filenumber1*. Then I can do it again. Each of these resource declarations will email me about the specified missing file. Using a defined type, I can compartmentalize and duplicate blocks of logic, similar to an instance class in most object-oriented languages:

```
define yellifmissing ($path) {
    exec { mailaboutit:
            command => "echo 'OhNoes!' | mail -s '$name is missing' admin@example.com",
            unless => "test -f $path",
            }
    }

yellifmissing { pathnumber1: path => '/tmp/filenumber1' }
yellifmissing { pathnumber2: path => '/tmp/filenumber2' }
```

Inheritance and Parameterized Classes

As we saw in the `ntp` example, classes are great for organizing our configurations, but they can also enhance the reusability of our code. Classes in Puppet, unlike define types, are not like their instanceable namesake in other object-oriented programming languages. They will take parameters and can even inherit structure from other classes, but only one class of a particular name can exist on each node.

We can build a base class that installs our Apache2 package and sets up a service to manage it. We can then inherit from the base and add a couple of special-purpose classes for an Apache with SSL and Apache with PHP. This helps to reduce duplication in our code and makes future changes less onerous:

```
class http-server {
    package { "apache2": ensure => installed }

    service { "apache2":
        ensure => running,
        enable => true,
        pattern => "apache2",
        subscribe => Package["apache2"],
        }
}

class https-server inherits http-server {
    exec { "a2enmod ssl":
        creates => "/etc/apache2/mods-enabled/ssl.load",
        notify => Service["apache2"],
        }
}

class http-php-server inherits http-server {
    package { "libapache2-mod-php5": ensure => installed }

    exec { "a2enmod php5":
        creates => "/etc/apache2/mods-enabled/php5.load",
        notify => Service["apache2"],
        }

    file { "/etc/php5/apache2/php.ini":
        source => "puppet:///modules/apps/php5/php.ini",
        notify => Service["apache2"],
        }
}
```

We can also pass parameters into classes when we include them in a node. Say we need to install different package versions on different systems. We can build a class that accepts a parameter $version and then passes that on to a package resource inside.

Here I've built a class called ruby that accepts a parameter named version that has a default value of '1.8'. Then I've declared the ruby class in my example node, passing the version '1.9.1'. If I omit the version parameter, the package will be installed with the default value, but I am otherwise allowed to override the version with whatever I choose:

```
class ruby ( $version = '1.8') {
    $package_list = ["ruby$version",
                     "ruby$version-dev",
                     "rubygems$version",
                     "libopenssl-ruby$version",]

    package { $package_list:
                    ensure =>installed,
        }
```

```
}

node "test.example.com" {
    class { 'apps::ruby':
        version => "1.9.1",
    }
}
```

 In the last example, I built an array of package names and passed them into a package resource. This is an example of a custom variable declaration.

Virtual Resources

Resources in Puppet can only be declared once per client configuration. This can make managing resources that relate to multiple configurations complicated. To alleviate this issue, we have the virtual resource. When marked with a @ prefix, a resource can be declared, but not yet applied to the client. When we want to apply it to a particular client, it must be realized first.

I've declared three virtual users: bob, alice, and eve, each of which has a different group membership. If I'd like to realize one of these users, I could use the realize User[*username*] mechanism. It could be tedious to realize each of your users in this fashion. In order to realize virtual resources in groups, specified by their attributes, we can use collections. The last two statements are collections; each is a collection of users defined by their membership in a particular group. The first collection will contain alice and eve and the second will contain all three:

```
@user { bob:
    ensure => present,
    groups => [ "mail", "web" ],
}

@user { alice:
    ensure => present,
    groups => [ "db", "web" ],
}

@user { eve:
    ensure => present,
    groups => [ "db", "web", "mail", "admin" ],
}

User <| group == db |>

User <| group == web |>
```

Variables

Variables are denoted by a $ prefix and can be declared as arrays or hashes. They can be scoped locally to a class or globally if declared outside a class. Class-scoped variables are also available publicly by qualifying their parent class:

```
class classone {
    $variableone = 'test'
    $variabletwo = [ 'foo', 'bar', 'baz', 'qux' ]
    $variablethree = { foo => 'bar', baz => 'qux' }

}
class classtwo {
    $variableone = $classone::variableone
    $variabletwo = $classone::variabletwo[1]
    $variablethree = $classtwo::variablethree[foo]
}
```

This can be useful in some circumstances, but it is somewhat difficult to ensure predictable behavior, as the values are dependent on the order of evaluation of the two classes. If you need to use a variable from one class in another, be sure that you can guarantee the order in which they are evaluated.

 Puppet also supports an extensive set of comparison and arithmetic operators (even Backus-Naur Form!) for expressions as variable values. See the Puppet language guide at *http://docs.puppetlabs.com/guides/language_guide.html* for complete documentation.

Resource Chaining

Managing the order that your resources execute in is one of the most important things you will do when writing a class. Unfortunately, the more complex and longer a class becomes, the harder it is to "see" those relationships. Chaining is a neat feature that can help clarify the dependencies. Both before/requires and notify type relationships can be specified by using directional arrows between the related classes.

In the first example, I've used a straight arrow to specify that the postgres package should be managed before its associated config file. In the next, the tilde arrow specifies that the postgres config file should notify the service. A more powerful feature is demonstrated on the last line, where a collection is used to specify that the rubygems package should be managed before any package that uses the gem provider. In this way, we can constuct concise one-to-many dependency between our managed gems and the gem program required:

```
Package['postgresql-8.4'] -> File ['/etc/postgresql/8.4/main/postgresql.conf']

File['/etc/postgresql/8.4/main/postgresql.conf'] ~> Service['postgres']
```

```
Package['rubygems'] -> Package <| provider == gem |>
```

 Resources can be chained on declaration, as well as by reference like in these examples. However, this will often make the declarations more confusing than using the alternative require or notify parameters.

Templates

Often you'll want to maintain configuration files for applications that are different between servers. If you have a couple of configurations, it's easy enough to maintain multiple files, but what if you have a very large number of differing configurations? We can manage this situation by writing ERB templates and populating the templates with node-specific information. This is done in Puppet with the template() function:

```
file { "apache-site":
    path => "/etc/apache2/sites-available/$fqdn",
    require => Package["apache2"],
    content => template("apache-site.erb"),
    notify => Exec["a2ensite"],
}

exec { "a2ensite $fqdn":
    notify => Service["apache2"],
    creates => "/etc/apache2/sites-enabled/$fqdn",
}
```

Here we have a file resource that creates an Apache config file named by the fqdn variable. We'll assume that Facter is populating this variable with the fully qualified domain name of our server. The file contents are generated by an ERB template and then it notifies an exec that enables the site and notifies Apache to restart. Next we'll write our template and place it in the expected location at /etc/puppet/templates/apache-site.erb:

```
<VirtualHost *:80>
    DocumentRoot /var/www/
    ServerName <%= name %>
    <Directory /var/www/>
        allow from all
        Options -Indexes
    </Directory>
</VirtualHost>
```

This is just a normal Apache vhost stanza, with the exception of the inline included name variable. All variables in the current scope are available to you in this manner and out-of-scope variables in other classes can be accessed by this lookupvar function, like so: scope.lookupvar('externalclass::myvariable'). Injecting variables into config file templates like this will let us drastically reduce the number of individual configuration files we need to maintain.

Documentation for the ERB templating system can be found at *http://www.ruby-doc.org/stdlib/libdoc/erb/rdoc/*, and there are plenty of online tutorials on complex templating.

I've tried to give you a few real-world examples of how to implement the various features of Puppet, but the applications are vast and varied. I suggest that you take a while to peruse the community repository of Puppet modules at *http://forge.puppetlabs.com/*. There are plenty of great patterns of implementation and organization in these projects, and you may even come across an out-of-the-box solution to a problem of your own.

## CHAPTER 3

Who Needs LDAP?

For many years I struggled with this question: "How do I effectively manage access control to Linux servers?" There are many options, including LDAP, Kerberos KDC, and the like, but I disliked each of them for one reason or another. Centralized auth is prone to failure and proper redundancy is painful to manage. Often password auth is well managed, but key distribution is difficult, or vice versa. With Puppet, I found a beautiful alternative. We can use Puppet to manage users and groups and distribute public keys. It can even enforce file and directory permissions and set password hashes. Gone are the days of writing big ugly scripts to push users and keys out to your whole farm of servers. We'll see how to accomplish this in a less painful manner using Puppet.

Building the Framework

First, we'll need a framework that can build user accounts in a repeatable fashion given a set of user attributes. We'll use a definition to make a reusable structure that can implement the user type repeatedly with different inputs.

There is a lot going on in this snippet, so I'll step through it point by point:

- We've set up a class called `rubyshadow` that declares a package resource to install `libshadow` for Ruby. This is a prerequisite that Puppet will need before it can manage passwords in the user type.

- Next we declare a define that takes a bunch of arguments describing our user and set a custom variable `$username` to the name of the resource, for clarity's sake.

- Then a user type declaration is made, passing the parameters from the define in to describe the user we want. The minimum member declaration specifies that the user can be a member of groups outside of this declaration and Puppet will not remove any groups added to the user manually.

- Finally, we ensure the ownership of the user's home and add the .ssh directory and populate the *authorized_keys*. This will allow us to manage the user's login credentials to our servers:

```
# modules/users/manifests/init.pp

# imports
import "people"

class rubyshadow {
    package { "libshadow-ruby1.8":
            ensure => installed,
    }
}

define useraccount ( $ensure = present, $uid, $pgroup = users,
$groups, $password, $fullname, $homefs, $shell ) {
    # Grab the username from the resource name
    $username = $name
    # define the user
    user { $username:
        ensure       => $ensure,
        uid          => $uid,
        gid          => $pgroup,
        groups       => $groups,
        listitemship => minimum,
        comment      => $fullname,
        home         => "${homefs}/$username",
        shell        => $shell,
        allowdupe    => false,
        password     => $password,
    }
    # Ensure the ownership and perms of the user home
    file { "${homefs}/${username}":
        ensure => directory,
        owner  => $home_owner,
        group  => $home_group,
        mode   => 750,
        require => User["${username}"],
    }
    # Create a dir for the ssh pubkey
    file { "${homefs}/${username}/.ssh":
        ensure => directory,
        owner  => $home_owner,
        group  => $home_group,
        mode   => 700,
        require => File["${homefs}/${username}"],
    }
    # Add the users pubkeys
    file { "${homefs}/${username}/.ssh/authorized_keys":
        ensure => present,
        owner  => $home_owner,
        group  => $home_group,
        mode   => 600,
        require => File["${homefs}/${username}/.ssh"],
        source => "puppet:///modules/users/${username}/.ssh/authorized_keys",
    }

}
```

Declaring Users

In this file, we've created a class called `people` that includes our `rubyshadow` class, sets up a couple of default values, and checks the home directory for sanity. Then we create a virtual resource named `alice` from our defined useraccount type. Alice has a couple of group memberships and her password parameter is supplied with a hash. This hash can either be mined out of a shadow file or generated with the `mkpasswd` utility. Bob is also present, and he's a member of the db group:

```
# modules/users/people.pp

class people {
    # include our rubyshadow class
    include rubyshadow
    # set some defaults
    $shell = "/bin/bash"
    $homefs = "/home"
    # make sure that /home is correct
    file { $homefs:
            ensure  => directory,
            owner   => "root",
            group   => "root",
            mode    => 2755
    }

    @useraccount { "alice":
        ensure   => "present",
        uid      => "1001",
        pgroup   => "users",
        groups   => ["db", "web", "admin"],
        fullname => "Alice",
        homefs   => $homefs,
        shell    => $shell,
        password => '$6$V38meAAms5qFW$iTXOEpsGGlWxqkVByPw75zF8QbVNMTLPyY8Hk6RykfTDR
                    cCTegRtjCpssZPJsUXRJJihgWHX.aOxaeuszjPiiO',
    }

    @useraccount { "bob":
        ensure   => "present",
        uid      => "1002",
        pgroup   => "users",
        groups   => ["db"],
        fullname => "Bob",
        homefs   => $homefs,
        shell    => $shell,
        password => '$6$CiljlJAsBzc.fm7Q$dloO/DsoVUD.MBeItUPrb8m5TkRmFSpQZP3smK9yTFV
                    dIyn4ib54PvohmkSn93WvPKUIXwODEUIjumCmsQ7rdO',
    }
}
```

I've made Alice and Bob virtual resources here, because I may not want to have user-accounts on all of my nodes. If I were to have declared a real resource, every node that includes the people class would have had her user created. This way, I can realize only the users in the web group on nodes *A.example.com* and both users in the web and db groups on *B.example.com*.

 It may seem obvious, but it must be said: Your Puppet manifests need to be kept secure. They will often contain secrets such as user password hashes and database credentials. Even if you can distribute those pieces out of band, the classes themselves are a road map to your system configuration and would be a security breach should they find a way out of your organization.

In this example, Alice will have an account on *A.example.com* and both Alice and Bob will have users created on *B.example.com*. In this way, we can distribute users with ssh keys and privilege credentials to our servers in a uniform and automated manner:

```
class webusers {
    Useraccount <| groups == "web" |>
    }
class dbusers {
    Useraccount <| groups == "db" |>
    }
node "A.example.com" {
    include webusers
    }
node "B.example.com" {
    include webusers
    include dbusers
    }
```

Throw Away the Handwritten Notebooks

Now that you've learned some Puppet and implemented an automation that does something useful, I'd like to talk about *what it all means* in the real world. Configuration management has been around for a long time, but its nature is changing. When we used to talk about configuration management, it involved checklists and difficult to test scripts. Often the policy documents regarding these topics were where 90% of the effort landed, and even those were not well adhered to. In the new structure that modern automation provides us, the system configuration can be treated like code. We can put it in version control, write functional testing suites for it, and QA it just like application releases. Configurations can have releases that relate to application code releases in meaningful ways, and bugs are easier to identify because we have explicit records of changes. So throw away the handwritten server log, and stop making cowboy changes to production servers. There is a better way.

## CHAPTER 4

MCollective

Puppet is not the end of this journey. We can abstract even further if we begin to talk about pools of servers and virtual instances. What if we have a cluster of application nodes that need to be managed as groups or if we need reporting of Facter variables from all of the nodes that include a certain Puppet class? What do we do if Apache needs a kick on 25 instances out of 1000? MCollective can do these things and more.

MCollective uses a publish/subscribe message bus to distribute commands to systems in parallel. It's used to push requests or commands out to all of your systems at once, allowing the MCollective server to decide which of the messages it should execute, based on a set of filters in the message. A good analogue of this is an IRC chat service. We can chat in a channel and receive all the messages, but messages that are intended for us will have our name attached to them.

The messages that an MCollective server consumes are then passed on to agent modules that consume the message parameters and then do some work. Agents exist for all sorts of behaviors, such as managing running services; running Puppet; managing packages, processes, and files; and even banning IP addresses with `iptables`. Beyond this, the agents are fairly simple to write using SimpleRPC.

Getting the Software

MCollective installation is not as simple as Puppet was. We need to set up a Stomp messaging server and configure the MCollective server on each of our hosts before we can start using it.

ActiveMQ

ActiveMQ is Apache's Java messaging server. We'll need to install the Sun Java Runtime, get the ActiveMQ package, and configure it. If you're running Ubuntu, the package `sun-java6-jre` can be downloaded from the partner repository. You can download an ActiveMQ tar from *http://activemq.apache.org/activemq-542-release.html*.

Once you have Java installed and the tarball extracted, you'll need to edit the *conf/activemq.xml* file and add some authentication details to it. I'll include an example below; the pertinent portions being the creation of an authorization user for MCollective and the MCollective topic. These are necessary to allow MCollective servers and client to talk to one another. You'll need these credentials for your MCollective configuration as well:

```
<!---- SNIP ----->

<plugins>
    <statisticsBrokerPlugin/>
    <simpleAuthenticationPlugin>
    <users>
    <authenticationUser username="mcollective" password="secrets"
        groups="mcollective,everyone"/>
    <authenticationUser username="admin" password="moresecrets"
        groups="mcollective,admin,everyone"/>
    </users>
    </simpleAuthenticationPlugin>
    <authorizationPlugin>
    <map>
    <authorizationMap>
        <authorizationEntries>
        <authorizationEntry queue=">" write="admins" read="admins" admin="admins" />
        <authorizationEntry topic=">" write="admins" read="admins" admin="admins" />
        <authorizationEntry topic="mcollective.>" write="mcollective"
            read="mcollective" admin="mcollective" />
        <authorizationEntry topic="mcollective.>" write="mcollective"
            read="mcollective" admin="mcollective" />
        <authorizationEntry topic="ActiveMQ.Advisory.>" read="everyone"
            write="everyone" admin="everyone"/>
        </authorizationEntries>
    </authorizationMap>
    </map>
    </authorizationPlugin>
</plugins>

<!---- SNIP ----->
```

You can now start up ActiveMQ with the command **bin/activemq start**.

MCollective Server

The MCollective "server" is the part that you'll need to deploy on all of your nodes. The client is a sort of command console that sends messages to the servers. The installation of MCollective itself is fairly straightforward and has packages available for most distributions. You'll need at least one client and one server installed in order to execute commands. Alternatively, there is a community Puppet module that can be used for installation of MCollective and distribution of the accompanying plug-ins:

- MCollective downloads: *http://www.puppetlabs.com/misc/download-options/*
- MCollective Puppet module: *https://github.com/mikepea/puppet-module-mcollective*

Once it's installed, you'll need to edit the */etc/mcollective/server.cfg* and */etc/mcollective/client.cfg* files, entering the MCollective user's password that you specified in the activemq configuration in the `plugin.stomp.password` field and specify your Stomp hostname in the `plugin.stomp.host` field. The *plugin.psk* secret must match between the server and client, as it is used for messaging encryption. This config assumes that you have Puppet installed and looks for the class file at the default location and sets the fact source to Facter:

```
# /etc/mcollective/server.cfg
topicprefix = /topic/mcollective
libdir = /usr/share/mcollective/plugins
logfile = /var/log/mcollective.log
loglevel = info
daemonize = 1

# Plugins
securityprovider = psk
plugin.psk = mysharedsecret

connector = stomp
plugin.stomp.host = stomp.example.com
plugin.stomp.port = 61613
plugin.stomp.user = mcollective
plugin.stomp.password = secret

# Facts
factsource = facter
# Puppet setup
classesfile = /var/lib/puppet/state/classes.txt

plugin.service.hasstatus = true
plugin.service.hasrestart = true
```

In order for the Facter fact source to work correctly, you will need to distribute the Facter plug-in for MCollective to the servers. The plug-in source can be fetched from GitHub at *https://github.com/puppetlabs/mcollective-plugins/tree/master/facts/facter/* and installed to the server under *$libdir/mcollective*. Remember to restart MCollective after copying the files so that MCollective will recognize the new agent.

MCollective Client

You'll need to install and configure the client in the same fashion. Here's an example of the client configuration:

```
topicprefix = /topic/mcollective
libdir = /usr/share/mcollective/plugins
logfile = /dev/null
```

```
loglevel = info

# Plugins
securityprovider = psk
plugin.psk = mysharedsecret

connector = stomp
plugin.stomp.host = stomp.example.com
plugin.stomp.port = 61613
plugin.stomp.user = mcollective
plugin.stomp.password = secret
```

 These configuration files contain secrets that can be used to publish commands onto the MCollective channel. The MCollective servers necessarily run as root and execute with full privileges. It is of utmost importance that access to the secrets and the Stomp server be carefully controlled.

MCollective Commands

With both the servers and a client configured, we're ready to start issuing MCollective commands. Let's start off with the mc-find-hosts command. When run without any argument, mc-find-hosts will list all of the MCollective servers that are currently active and listening:

```
:> mc-find-hosts
A.example.com
B.example.com
C.example.com
D.example.com
```

We can also get some information about our individual MCollective nodes. mc-inventory will tell us what agents are available on a node, what Puppet classes that node is a member of, and assuming the Facter module is installed, a list out all of the available Facter facts about the node:

```
:> mc-inventory A.example.com

Inventory for A.example.com:

Server Statistics:
    Version: 1.0.1
    Start Time: Fri May 06 11:10:34 -0700 2011
    Config File: /etc/mcollective/server.cfg
    Process ID: 22338
    Total Messages: 143365
    Messages Passed Filters: 75428
    Messages Filtered: 67937
    Replies Sent: 75427
    Total Processor Time: 162.09 seconds
    System Time: 73.08 seconds
```

```
Agents:
    discovery      filemgr      package
    iptables       nrpe         rpcutil
    process        puppetd
    service

Configuration Management Classes:
    ntp            php                   apache2
    mysql-5            varnish

Facts:
    architecture => x86_64
    domain => example.com
    facterversion => 1.5.7
    fqdn => A.example.com
    hostname => A
    id => root
    is_virtual => true
    kernel => Linux
    kernelmajversion => 2.6
    kernelversion => 2.6.35
```

This is already a useful tool for diagnostics and inventory on all of your Puppet-managed servers, but MCollective also lets us execute agents on the target systems, filtered by any of these attributes, facts, agents, or classes. For example, if our servers run Apache and we need to restart all of the Apaches on all of our servers, we could use the mc-service agent to do this:

```
:> mc-service --with-class apache2 apache2 restart
```

This will place a message on the MCollective message bus that says: "All the servers with the apache2 Puppet class, use your service agent to restart apache2." We can even add multiple filters like the following:

```
:> mc-service --with-class apache2 --with-fact architecture=x86_64 apache2 restart
```

This will let us restart Apache on only the 64bit "x86_64" architecture servers that have the Puppet apache2 class. These sorts of filters make remote execution of tasks on particular subsets of servers very easy.

Of particular interest to those of us running large infrastructures is MCollective's built-in capacity to run the Puppet agent on the servers. Puppet's client-server model, in its default configuration, will poll the Puppet Master once every half hour. This is not convenient, for instance, if you would like to use Puppet to coordinate an application release on a group of servers. If you would like some control over the sequence and timing of the Puppet runs, you can use the MCollective puppetd agent and forgo the polling behavior of the agent daemon. Since Puppet is built in to MCollective, it is not necessary to run the agent on boot either. So long as MCollective and Puppet are both installed, we can execute Puppet as we like.

The agent can be downloaded from GitHub at *https://github.com/puppetlabs/mcollec tive-plugins/tree/master/agent/puppetd/* and, as with the Facter plug-in, should be copied to *$libdir/mcollective* on the servers, preferably using Puppet. Once it's installed, you will be able to kick off a Puppet run on all or some of your servers with the following command:

```
:> mc-puppetd --with-class example runonce
```

If you don't mind the default polling behavior of the Puppet agent, you can also use the puppetd MCollective agent to selectively enable or disable Puppet on sets of your instances as well as initiate one-off runs of the agent.

 If you still want to have Puppet run on a regular basis to ensure configuration correctness, but need to avoid polling "stampedes," take a look at the PuppetCommander project at *http://projects.puppetlabs.com/projects/mcollective-plugins/wiki/ToolPuppetcommander*. It uses MCollective's puppetd module to centrally coordinate Puppet runs so as to avoid overwhelming a Puppet Master. It will also give you the power to specify which nodes or classes to run automatically.

Finally, there is an mc-rpc command that serves as a sort of metacommand, allowing access to all of the available agents. We can execute the puppetd agent, for example, with the following syntax:

```
:> mc-rpx --agent puppetd --with-class example runonce
```

Alternatively, we can use mc-rpc to read out the documentation for a particular agent:

```
:> mc-rpc --agent-help puppetd
SimpleRPC Puppet Agent
======================

Agent to manage the puppet daemon

     Author: R.I.Pienaar
     Version: 1.3-sync
     License: Apache License 2.0
     Timeout: 120
Home Page: http://mcollective-plugins.googlecode.com/


ACTIONS:
========
disable, enable, runonce, status

disable action:
---------------
     Disables the Puppetd

     INPUT:

     OUTPUT:
         output:
```

```
            Description: String indicating status
            Display As: Statc
runonce action:
---------------
    Initiates a single Puppet run

    INPUT:

    OUTPUT:
        output:
            Description: Output from puppetd
            Display As: Output

status action:
--------------
    Status of the Puppet daemon

    INPUT:

    OUTPUT:
        enabled:
            Description: Is the agent enabled
            Display As: Enabled

        lastrun:
            Description: When last did the agent run
            Display As: Last Run

        output:
            Description: String displaying agent status
            Display As: Status

        running:
            Description: Is the agent running
            Display As: Running
```

You've seen the basic features of MCollective in this chapter. It works as a great orchestration tool for Puppet, allowing you greater control over your Puppet agents and more insight into your configurations through Facter. Beyond this, the agents are fairly simple to write and can be used to accomplish any task that you might want to execute in a distributed fashion across all or part of your infrastructure. Puppet Labs provides documentation on extending MCollective with custom agents with SimpleRPC at *http://docs.puppetlabs.com/mcollective/simplerpc/agents.html*.

## CHAPTER 5

Puppetry with Friends

The necessary development environment for testing Puppet manifests can be difficult to maintain even when you're working alone. What happens when you have a whole archive of classes with dependencies and multiple uses? Some of those classes are bound to be running on production equipment, and several engineers will need to work on features and fixes simultaneously. The need for a lifecycle with development, staging, and production environments quickly becomes urgent.

Environments

Puppet allows you to create environments with different manifest files for modules, nodes, and templates. In order to start using this feature, you'll need to create a new set of modules, manifests, and templates directories in a subdirectory of */etc/puppet* on the Puppet Master and then specify their location in a new stanza in your *puppet.conf* as follows:

```
[development]

modulepath = $confdir/environments/development/modules
manifest = $confdir/environments/development/manifests/site.pp
templatedir = $confdir/environments/development/templates
```

Once you've put some usable code in these directories, you can specify the new development for use on an agent node by either passing **--environment development** to pup petd on invocation, or by placing a new parameter in the agent's *puppet.conf* [agent] stanza:

```
[agent]
  environment = development
```

Now we can tinker to our heart's content without risk of breaking production configurations. If you have taken to the practice of keeping your configurations in version control (I use git), this can be taken a step further. Just as you might use a branching strategy to manage the workflow of development projects with multiple contributors, you can also use a branching strategy with your Puppet repository. A simple technique for this involves creating a branch for each environment. For instance, I would check out my development repository branch into the development environment directory specified by the appropriate environment definition in *puppet.conf*. I could then create and check out a production and staging branch into their matching environments as well.

I recommend starting with a simple set of branches for development, testing, and production definitions. If your team is large enough for a single development branch to have a confusing amount of change, it may benefit you to switch to a per-contributor or per-feature branching strategy. Branching and versioning strategies are a source of great discourse and contention, so I'll lean away from any philisophical prescription here and just advise that you should use what works.

Reporting

Once you have Puppet running in an automated fashion on a number of servers, it becomes fairly important to begin tracking what is happening and when. A default Puppet Master configuration will output plenty of information in the system logs, but this isn't terribly convenient for archiving or monitoring's sake.

Puppet provides a reporting tool for keeping track of its run results. There are several output types for these reports. The simplest is configured by setting the **report = file** parameter in [master] stanza of your *puppet.conf* on the Puppet Master. This will cause Puppet to output a run log each time it is executed and save the result in */var/lib/puppet/reports/agent.example.com* on the Puppet Master. This will generate a readable, but generally very verbose YAML file on every run.

A more featureful way to inspect your reports is provided with the Puppet Labs "Dashboard." Dashboard is a Rails application that functions as a report processor and presents an easy to understand arrangement of graphs and report results that makes managing large numbers of Puppet agent instances simpler.

The simplest way to get started with the Dashboard on Ubuntu is with the Puppet Labs apt repository packages. In order to add the repository, place the following content in a file at */etc/apt/sources.list.d/puppetlabs.list*. You may need to replace oneiric with your current ubuntu version codename:

```
# Puppet Labs Repository
deb http://apt.puppetlabs.com/ubuntu oneiric main
deb-src http://apt.puppetlabs.com/ubuntu oneiric main
```

Run the following commands to install the Dashboard from the repository:

```
sudo apt-get update; sudo apt-get install puppet-dashboard
```

The Dashboard also requires a MySQL server in order to store and index the report results. To install MySQL, run **sudo apt-get install mysql-server**. Record the root password that you create in the installation prompt. Next, run **mysql -u root -p** and execute the following SQL to create a user for the Dashboard:

```
CREATE DATABASE dashboard CHARACTER SET utf8;
CREATE USER 'dashboard'@'localhost' IDENTIFIED BY 'password';
GRANT ALL PRIVILEGES ON dashboard.* TO 'dashboard'@'localhost';
```

You'll also need to configure */etc/puppet-dashboard/database.yml* with the credentials that you've just created. The following example will work with the user creation commands in the last example:

```
production:
  database: dashboard
  username: dashboard
  password: password
  encoding: utf8
  adapter: mysql
```

Now create the Dashboard database, using the following commands to invoke the Rails rake process:

```
cd /usr/share/puppet-dashboard
sudo rake RAILS_ENV=production db:migrate
```

Once the database is created, you can uncomment the START=yes statement in */etc/default/puppet-dashboard* and */etc/default/puppet-dashboard-worker*. To start up the dashboard, execute the following commands:

```
sudo service puppet-dashboard start; sudo service puppet-dashboard-workers-start
```

The Dashboard application will now be available at *http://localhost:3000*, but it will be quite empty of reports. To start sending reports to your Dashboard, you will need to add the appropriate configuration to your Puppet Master's */etc/puppet.conf*. The configuration as follows should work if your Dashboard shares a server with the Puppet Master. Otherwise, you will need to enter the appropriate hostname rather than local host:

```
reports = http
reporturl = http://localhost:3000/reports/upload
```

Once your Puppet Master is reporting to the Dashboard, you should start seeing reports show up shortly after a Puppet agent completes a run. Each run appears in the central list with an icon indicating whether it succeeded without changes, succeeded with changes, or failed. Clicking on the host will let you drill down into what changes were made or errors were reported. The Dashboard gives you an easy way to gauge the health of your system and identify failing configurations at a glance.

Version control commit tags can be added to your reports by adding the following parameter to the [master] of your Puppet Master's */etc/puppet/puppet.conf*:

```
config_version = 'git --git-dir /etc/puppet/.git rev-parse\
                   --short HEAD 2>/dev/null || echo'
config_version = 'svn info /etc/puppet/ | grep Revision:
                  | egrep -o [0-9]+'
```

## CHAPTER 6

Extending Puppet

When you are tackling a complicated configuration deployment with Puppet, you may find yourself wishing for a feature that doesn't exist. Sometimes you need a piece of information that is not available to you until runtime. I will use an example here that I've encountered in an application deployment.

My own use of Puppet tends to be on the Amazon Web Services Cloud. This leads me to want to integrate some of the metadata from Amazon's API into Puppet. In one particular case, I wanted to use the tagging API to decide which instances my HAProxy configuration would balance. Amazon's tagging API allows me to associate arbitrary key-value metadata "tags" with AWS resources such as machine instances. If Puppet could talk to Amazon and derive the appropriate connection strings of all the servers with a particular tag, it would greatly simplify my life!

Custom Functions

By creating a custom function in Puppet, we are adding logic to the parsing step of the manifest compilation. The function can be called in our Puppet manifests and will be executed on the Puppet Master before communicating the compiled catalog to the agent. This means that we can use these functions to make decisions or import information from external sources, but we cannot use them to directly alter the agent host.

In my case I want to fetch some information from the AWS REST API and return it so that I can put the values in my HAProxy configuration file. I'll start by adding a directory to my Puppet configuration tree at *modules/ec2/lib/puppet/parser/functions*. I've created a new module called `ec2`, and I'll put my custom function where the Puppet Master expects to find such things, in *lib/puppet/parser/functions*.

Now I'll create a file in the functions directory called *getIPsByTag.rb* and require the fog gem. I'm going to use the fog gem to reduce the work I have to do to integrate with the AWS API. A new function is defined by calling the `newfunction` method in the `Puppet::Parser::Functions` module and passing the name of the new function as a symbol and the function type. There are two function types. The "statement" type will execute but return no result and the "rvalue" type will return a value so that it can be used in a decision or assignment context. This function will be of the type "rvalue" and will accept the arguements "key" and "value" while returning a hash of the matching instance IDs and private IP addresses:

```
require 'rubygems'
require 'fog'

module Puppet::Parser::Functions
  newfunction(:getIPsByTag, :type => :rvalue) do |args|
    filter = { 'key' => args[0] }
    filter = { 'value' => args[1] }
    instances  = {}

    Fog.credentials_path = '/etc/puppet/fog_cred'

    # new compute provider from AWS
    compute = Fog::Compute.new(:provider => 'AWS')

    # print resource id's by the hash {key => value}
    compute.describe_tags(filter).body['tagSet'].each do|tag|
      instance_desc = compute.describe_instances('instance-id' => tag['resourceId'])
      instance_facts = instance_desc.body['reservationSet'][0]['instancesSet'][0]
      instances[tag['resourceId']] = instance_facts['privateIpAddress']
    end

    return instances

  end
end
```

My logic in this function makes a call to describe the tags matching the filter that we passed in and then fetches the IP addresses of those instances in the next call, pushing the values of the instance ID and associated IP address into the returned hash. That was fast and fairly simple to implement; now let's see how to use it.

Below is my haproxy class. I install the application from the distribution package and use a template to generate a config file from that big list of parameters that is passed in at the top:

```
class haproxy($proxies,$health_host,$health_uri,$health_inter,$backend_port) {
  package { "haproxy": ensure => installed }

  file { "/etc/haproxy/haproxy.cfg":
          content => template("apps/haproxy/haproxy.cfg.erb"),
          require => Package[haproxy];
        "/etc/default/haproxy":
          content => 'ENABLED=1',
          require => Package[haproxy];
  }

  service { "haproxy":
        ensure => running,
        hasstatus => true,
```

```
            enable => true,
            subscribe => [Package["haproxy"],
                          File["/etc/haproxy/haproxy.cfg", "/etc/default/haproxy"]
                          ],
    }

}
```

Let's examine the pertinent parts of the configuration template. The template expects that there will be a variable in the class called **proxies** containing our defined servers, each with another hash of their backend's ID and IPs:

```
# Set up application listeners here.
<% proxies.each do |listener,backend_hash| -%>
listen application <%= listener %>
option httpchk GET <%= health_uri %> HTTP/1.1\r\nHost:\ <%= health_host %>
option forwardfor

<% backend_hash.each do |id,ip| -%>
  server <%= id %> <%= ip %>:<%= backend_port %> check inter <%= health_inter %>
<% end -%>

<% end -%>
```

Let's define our node and get the right data into this class. As you can see below, I've defined a **proxies** hash containing our listener definitions and the key and then calling getIPsByTag() to define the hash of the backend values:

```
node "haproxy.example.com" {
  class { 'haproxy':
    proxies => { '0.0.0.0:8000' => getIPsByTag('app-type', 'tomcat'),
                 '0.0.0.0:8001' => getIPsByTag('app-type', 'rails)'
               },
    health_host => 'example.com',
    health_uri => '/',
    health_inter => 10000,
    backend_port => 8080,
  }
}
```

And finally, the resulting *haproxy.cf*:

```
listen application 0.0.0.0:8000
option httpchk GET / HTTP/1.1\r\nHost:\ example.com
option forwardfor

  server i-dc4d30bc 10.101.43.255:8080 check inter 10000
  server i-cv443dbe 10.101.42.254:8080 check inter 10000

listen application 0.0.0.0:8001
option httpchk GET / HTTP/1.1\r\nHost:\ example.com
option forwardfor

  server i-dc0h30cc 10.111.44.254:8080 check inter 10000
  server i-ec0b69cc 10.111.42.255:8080 check inter 10000
```

Now I can tag an instance and be assured that it will be added to my application pool automatically on the next Puppet run. This example may or may not be useful to your particular needs, but I hope it demonstrates clearly how simple it is to integrate outside data sources or custom logic into your Puppet manifests.

About the Author

James Loope is the operations lead at Janrain. He is a specialist in scalable infrastructure, virtualization, cloud infrastructure, and computer security.

Colophon

The animal on the cover of *Managing Infrastructure with Puppet* is an English setter.

The cover image is from *Wood's Animate Creations*. The cover font is Adobe ITC Garamond. The text font is Linotype Birka; the heading font is Adobe Myriad Condensed; and the code font is LucasFont's TheSansMonoCondensed.

Get even more for your money.

Join the O'Reilly Community, and register the O'Reilly books you own. It's free, and you'll get:

- $4.99 ebook upgrade offer
- 40% upgrade offer on O'Reilly print books
- Membership discounts on books and events
- Free lifetime updates to ebooks and videos
- Multiple ebook formats, DRM FREE
- Participation in the O'Reilly community
- Newsletters
- Account management
- 100% Satisfaction Guarantee

Signing up is easy:

1. Go to: oreilly.com/go/register
2. Create an O'Reilly login.
3. Provide your address.
4. Register your books.

Note: English-language books only

To order books online:
oreilly.com/store

For questions about products or an order:
orders@oreilly.com

To sign up to get topic-specific email announcements and/or news about upcoming books, conferences, special offers, and new technologies:
elists@oreilly.com

For technical questions about book content:
booktech@oreilly.com

To submit new book proposals to our editors:
proposals@oreilly.com

O'Reilly books are available in multiple DRM-free ebook formats. For more information:
oreilly.com/ebooks

O'REILLY®

Spreading the knowledge of innovators | oreilly.com

The information you need, when and where you need it.

With Safari Books Online, you can:

Access the contents of thousands of technology and business books

- Quickly search over 7000 books and certification guides
- Download whole books or chapters in PDF format, at no extra cost, to print or read on the go
- Copy and paste code
- Save up to 35% on O'Reilly print books
- **New!** Access mobile-friendly books directly from cell phones and mobile devices

Stay up-to-date on emerging topics before the books are published

- Get on-demand access to evolving manuscripts.
- Interact directly with authors of upcoming books

Explore thousands of hours of video on technology and design topics

- Learn from expert video tutorials
- Watch and replay recorded conference sessions

Spreading the knowledge of innovators   safari.oreilly.com

Lightning Source UK Ltd.
Milton Keynes UK
UKHW051413090721
386897UK00004B/237